Praise for *how to make a basket*

'Within the pages of this crackling debut collection, Jazz Money guides us through the steps on *how to make a basket*, a learning seeped in a deep respect for Country; her heart and veins, her soil and spirit. Poetry sings and calls to us on every page, within each line, sometimes quietly, but also with roaring energy. I adore this book, and will cherish having learnt from Jazz Money that it takes true love to make a great poem.'

Tony Birch

'*how to make a basket* is a lesson written on the body, navigating contours and flows on Country, awakenings and flesh; a delicate constellation of strands reflecting rivers and stars, spilling moonglow and song on the pulse of time. This is a fierce and intimate offering storied through blood and secrets and salt and ash; an exquisite weave of pleasure and pain to carry heartbeats and truths, gifted to ancestors and her every horizon.'

Natalie Harkin

'This is a brilliant debut that leaps, lights and lives in tune with the depths of love. Satirical, sensitive and subversive, Jazz Money is a poet to watch.'

Omar Sakr

'Jazz Money rebirths the art of storytelling in *how to make a basket* ⋯⋯⋯⋯⋯⋯ of language and time, echoing the line⋯

Yvette Holt

'A luminous and beautifully sculpted, seamless collection of poems that reflects on place and passion. *how to make a basket* builds on the growing canon of work by contemporary Indigenous women poets, yet offers a new, fresh perspective on remembering and forgetting.'

2020 David Unaipon Award Judges

Jazz Money is a poet and artist of Wiradjuri heritage, currently based on sovereign Gadigal land. Her poetry has been published widely and reimagined as murals, installations, digital interventions and film. Jazz's poetry has been recognised with the David Unaipon Award, the Aunty Kerry Reed-Gilbert Poetry Prize, the University of Canberra Aboriginal and Torres Strait Islander Poetry Prize, a Copyright Agency First Nations Fellowship and a First Nations Emerging Career Award from the Australia Council for the Arts. *how to make a basket* is her first book.

JAZZ MONEY

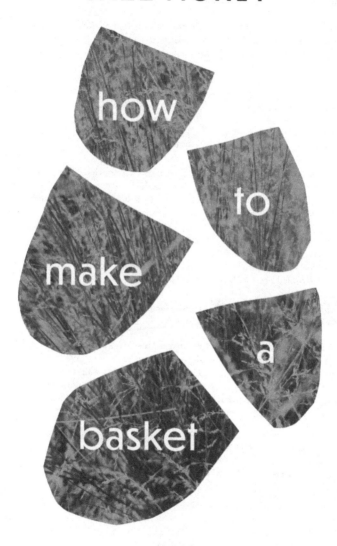

how

to

make

a

basket

UQP

First published 2021 by University of Queensland Press
PO Box 6042, St Lucia, Queensland 4067 Australia
Reprinted 2021 (twice), 2022, 2023

University of Queensland Press (UQP) acknowledges the Traditional Owners and
their custodianship of the lands on which UQP operates. We pay our respects to their
Ancestors and their descendants, who continue cultural and spiritual connections to
Country. We recognise their valuable contributions to Australian and global society.

uqp.com.au
reception@uqp.com.au

Cover design and photograph by Jenna Lee
Author photograph by Hannah Leser
Typeset in 11.5/14 pt Bembo Std by Post Pre-press Group, Brisbane
Printed in Australia by McPherson's Printing Group

State Library of Queensland

Queensland Government

University of Queensland Press (UQP) launched the David Unaipon Award
for an Emerging Aboriginal and/or Torres Strait Islander Writer in 1988.
Presented as part of the Queensland Literary Awards, in partnership with
State Library of Queensland, UQP is proud to publish the annual award-winning
manuscript, and is committed to building the profile of, and access to, Indigenous
writing in Australia and internationally.

Australian Government

Australia Council for the Arts

University of Queensland Press is
assisted by the Australian Government
through the Australia Council, its arts
funding and advisory body.

A catalogue record for this book is available from the National Library of Australia.

ISBN 978 0 7022 6338 5 (pbk)
ISBN 978 0 7022 6521 1 (epdf)

University of Queensland Press uses papers that are natural, renewable and recyclable
products made from wood grown in well-managed forests and other controlled sources.
The logging and manufacturing processes conform to the environmental regulations of
the country of origin.

For the matriarchs.

For those who fight for justice.

For my wife.

gulgandara
before

sweet smoke   3
gadi   6
as we attack   8
gununga   10
to fanny cochrane smith   14
gully song   15
listen   19
we rise   21
if I write a poem   23
ngargan   27

guray-dyu-ngi-nya
longing

redbellyblacksnake   31
false gods   32
dripping banksia pods   34
touchable   36
heaven sent   37
yirawulin   38
stormgirl   40
moreton bay fig   41
phosphorescence   42
old scars   43
our weak constellations   44
needles   46
ripples   47
echoes   48
into the moonlight, away from me   50
pepper   51
a blue morning   52
gudyi   54

guwiiny-ngali-gin-dyi
away from here

bila, a river cycle	59
through the moon	64
scatter gems	67
my grandmother's spirit	68
/ unprecedented times / 2020	70
a case study of the colony	72
keep in touch	74
my hand is a bird	78
smoke of the middens	79
a woman quaking	80
galaxies and nothing at all	81
salvation of the new world	83
let us suppose	84
bushfire love	86
a cab, early morning, in the rain	88
oil afloat at birrarung marr	89
I don't sleep anymore	90

ngulumunggu
endings

digital native 95

time travel 96

the transit of venus 98

on sun-days 102

desert places 103

prayer is electric 104

the young men are singing 108

hot and cold 109

the space between the paperbark 111

apathy 112

that shore which is a cliff 113

how to make a basket 114

notes 118

mandaang guwu, thank you 121

gulgandara

before

sweet smoke

it starts

               with smoke
it always starts   with smoke

mothers burred at the belly

        swollen as the great trees
come to

               this place
painted and slow
with a gasping gift

        canopy medicine
to welcome

        the person on hands and knees
           whose new blood makes magic

                  makes the earth anew
the grunting sweat almost terror

        turns to

                    bliss

      as sweet cries
wake the bush wake first eyes
sweated face becomes pure

            like rain
            like daybreak

when the world shifts

           from two set
wet heartbeats the wet orange womb glow

           to bright white light

and the gasping bub of day
                                        break cries
there is white smoke

to clear the bush to cleanse the air to welcome
wrinkled and furled
                                as a new leaf
sweet medicine
                        in the coolamon
                        carried wet and green
and old hands
            born here too
know the way to ash tie belly knots
            clever hands
                        don't forget   this place
where life begins

tell it to the bubs to pass on to theirs
                        when strangers come
                        when other trees fall

here in a vast hollow medicine tree
this is where life begins
            a tree so great
            a memory so long
can feel the way the air   has changed

hard rivers have formed in this bush
            black flat tar
where great steel fish swim

                    smoke turned dirty

and the river of destruction
                                    comes closer

white hands white hats white clipboards
                avert their   gaze from her
marked on the maps
                            to bring death here
                                    to a place of life
                    so it starts new
with smoke
            and familiar camp fire
sweet smoke
different but safe

                            textures change and
                            so do the tongues
the old words return

                                    medicine remembered
                            fires built the proper way

she waits   she sighs
remembers the thousand hands she birthed here
            and sees them return
carrying ancestors
carrying bubs

return with smoke
                    to keep her safe

gadi

I float translucent
upon
within the river
whisper home three times
ngurambang ngurambang ngurambang

★

a snake appears
beyond my skin it watches
though
this snake is made of sky

gadi I ask
are you real
gadi responds

waiting
I become another

★   the river is star sky country
bilabang
as we gaze below
our ancestors gaze deeper above

from within the snakes
tip   toe
ribcage
I am small
and the world is only made of dark

we wind
gadi carves me home
ngurambang ngurambang ngurambang

★

water tells a secret slowly
a snake listens as water

★

as gadi we gather
grasses leaves small sweet shoots
in my soft mouth
I carry careful
spreading seeds along a river home
bila
every seed a forest
to make more water
from which old bodies rise

★

slowly curve
slowly listen
all this will take
medicine
smoke
and time

★

do you hear that sound
it's the stars singing down
ngurambang ngurambang ngurambang

★ ★ ★   ★

as we attack

as we attack

                    in forward motion

                fish nimble fingers covered
                        in scales his wife

\

            wades alone
                    cold mornings

                            wet grasses carefully knotted
our lives on separate tides

                    that pull our scales apart
not chain mail

                    \

                                but soft flesh beneath
            flesh that moves and bends

his callused edges
                        and salt hair white flecks

8

around lips and eyes
        she collects and moves with the tides

\

        we do not bump together
like boats in the sheltered harbour

        tectonic plates move
        down your spine

trace the line where fish swim
        breathe in scales

        following underground channels
        to that inland sea

we exhale salt
        in forward motion

        she breathes in

        \

        holds back the tide

gununga

gabin-gidyal (beginning)

there is no beginning
not in that way
but some people
those who don't understand
begin where it ends where it changes

galabarra (in half)

begin
at the time
when the world split

wumba (evening star)

of all the stars
and the many eyes of ancestors
there is one to be followed
to spill blood
an excuse
venus a goddess to guide
burnt into the sky
a mother of war
followed by a rotting ship of men
to tahiti
some scientific excuse
to know the size of the unknowable

gabaa (strangers)

with whips and hands that snatch and steal
touch the flesh on islands
that are not their home
spreading a plague upon the tides

nirin (edge)

> upon the ship
> glittering instruments
> maps shaky and blurred
> no fill and all edges
> the ship falls from high

yiray (sun)

> the strangers assemble glass and shining metals
> attempt to calculate the sky
> but captain and his couldn't figure venus across the sun
> a false passage

guwanguwan (bloody)

> under red seal red wax

mugugalurgarra (keep secret)

> in ink impure read the words
> search between tahiti and new zealand
> for a continent or land of great extent

gibirrgan (southern cross)

> it begins to shift
> a sky on fire
> stars can be followed by others too
> storms and reefs gather

bunun (carried by wind)

> across great seas
> that hulking sickness comes

wambunbunmarra (greed)

> the first steps
> the first theft
> first shots
> first to run

madhu (enemy)

the first ones on the eastern shore

bangal-guwal-bang
(belonging to another place)

the first to burn
the first taken
worth collecting behind glass
on far strange shores
yet made by hands deemed disposable

yaambuldhaany (liar)

terra nullius
an empty land
where flag and steel grow as new feet step
the poison spreads from here

giyalang (belonging)

evening star
seen by all
venus a mother whose seeing brings tears
where here it was enough
to care and be cared
to belong within those stars

gununga (hiding inside)

many skies exist in the same night
those that hold all of time
old people and people not yet here
and a map hidden inside a home always known
followed by strangers to lead a darker sky
transit for glory
without a captured star
but many stars taken

giyira (future, the womb)

there is no end
not in that way
a shift within
an unbroken forever
all mapped there in those stars
those stars that could never be taken

to Fanny Cochrane Smith, to whale breath

the wail scratched
brittle wax to carry that
forever song
thank you colonisers
for remembering not to

sharing breath
a whale inhales far up coast
carries new air
to depth
for depth
breath held
imbued atmosphere
whale air
air wail
held time
held place
shared
brought breath
exhaled as mist
mist to breathe
a shared breath
breaching whale

forget the
last?

born upon that
blown upon island
(wax in their ears
to deafen the whales'
slaughter song)
mourning paths
on ocean floors forgotten
scrub track rock steps
old path
not forgotten
(whisper) taken torn stolen

air caught out of the wax
then upon
now-time ears

an island from breath
preserved
the wail
a great hidden river
to now
and many small songs
and many great whales

gully song

a mist seeps
through   this gully
        and I can hear

                        song
feel smoke cling to
        hair   to lashes
hear the way
the old voices are
                held here
        hold here

the way they have
                turned   to mist
that clings to
        the new shoots
the streaking old gums
to dawn to dew to breath

                        held

suspended on

                spider webs

song and smoke and words
                of air

                                /

there are birds   pinned
        to the sky
a great emu

                to guide us home

a good fire will
          trickle
                    across the land
                              like water
the old trees remember
whisper
          of our people
who have been   here
                    since the
                    first sunrise

of dance and feast
bodies tended with ground paints
          fine oils sweet medicine

the time before
          the smoke turned foul

/

          in this place

plastic plaques tell of

                              people
                              moved
of homes made with
          kerosene can walls
cold winters jobs with no pay

the plaques tell of bravery and
courage

of   hearts
broken anew

              of babies stolen

              tears that washed
the gully away

                    /
the plaques say nothing of the

                              songs
              I can hear
       held in the trees
                    in the mist

that haven't forgotten   aren't lost

       still walk here
              are still heard

/

              here now
on a Saturday   June   2019
       I see gunyas
              built this morning
by hands relearning   the old ways
       trees releasing
              new homes

and the gentle drip of the ferns
        sounds like
                    resilience
the mist loudest under the trees
           like bird song through rain

          /

    as I write
        this
orange face and orange breast
two   king parrots
    land in the mist
perch on a small gunya
        and pass a branch
        from
           beak to
           beak

.

listen

Country speaks Country sings
a heartbeat —

                                            listen

rivers have dried up
they are life and —

                                            listen

bush has been burnt
that's habitat
that's home
and this is urgent —

                                            listen

that silence speaks
of all those kin
and yet —

                                            listen

do you hear
the voices of ancestors
do you hear
the way the world was created
do you —

                                            listen

there are fists raised
there are voices singing
there are voices chanting
you must —

                                            listen

no more deaths
no more police

no more foreign laws
on sovereign soil –

                                        listen

no more kids taken
no more families broken –

                                        listen

this always was
this always will be
do you understand
this always was
this always will be –

                                        listen

pay attention
do you
understand
do you –

                                        listen

we rise

it used to be all
        white men shit
when I turned on the news
when I was little it was the same
                shitty white liberal prime minister shit
                shitty pauline hanson shit
                shitty gap that needed closin
        shitty fear of blak black brown
        of women
of people fleeing wars that we'd started
                I never thought I'd put pauline in a poem

HEY AUNTY P
YOU SEE US NOW

        we got a Blak Prime Minister
she's deadly
she's hot pink hot stuff   she brings her tiddas
                      and they love us
        they whip their hair
        kiss the bubs
it's all different now

        they dreamt up this future
                   and invited us with em
turns out the future is technicolour blak black brown
turns out we're all welcome here

queer brothers and sisters and non-binary siblings
if you been here since always
or if you come here now   just now
come here heart open
come here hurt from those wars
and those sea levels rising
my Prime Minister believes in us
she believes in me
wants our jarjums safe and educated good ways
wants the tiddas safe and the fellas too
she don't care if we rich and her cabinet don't either

I stand proud under our flag
lilac lime fuchsia
I stand proud
cos when Aunty Maya wrote
still I rise
I know she was thinking of us hey
all of us
blak black brown

if I write a poem

if I write a poem
it's for the pen
banned from my grandmother's hands

and if I write
it's for our language
stolen from the mouths
of babies in cribs

and if I write a poem
it's so that our children
will read some truth
of their family

and if I write
it's because our story
hasn't been written
                by us
                for us

and if I write
it's because I hate the structure
the capitalism
the greed
the fury

I write a poem
because I love this Country

I write a word
because I love my daughter
        who isn't yet born

I write because there is no truth yet
no justice

and if I write a poem
it's because my mother can't understand
why I weep into the soil
but she cries with me all the same

and if I write
it's because I love a woman
and others do
and cannot write about their love

and if I write a word
it's to stop me from burning
within
it's to stop me from burning
the city down
and baring my breasts
wailing with my clapsticks
a song that boils in my chest
in my soul
that no one has taught me the words to
yet

I write a poem
because I was raised off Country
and I yearn and yearn for a place I don't hold
that holds me

and if I don't write a poem
it's for the magnificence of lightning
of cicadas in chorus
            rhythms too beautiful to capture

and if I don't write a word
it's because I love this Country
and all the ways I love her burns
            all the ways I love her burns

and if I don't write
it's because I love a woman
and that is a sacred thing

if I don't write a word
it's because my mother loves me
every way she can

and if I don't write
it's because I can't bring my baby
into a world on fire

and if I don't write
don't think I have nothing to say
        if I don't write
        don't think I have nothing to say

and if I don't write
it's because this language
these letters
are not worthy

and if I write a word
on the inside of my mouth
in the dust
in the sand
it's because I know
no other truth at all

ngargan

when i break through the confines of english
i'm free

all the best things i write
are straining at the edges
of the coloniser's language

guray-dyu-ngi-nya

longing

redbellyblacksnake

the first time I knew
I would hold you always
a mother
        red belly black snake
glided by
as we loved
underneath the eyes of the Illawarra
        blessing us
she was all fertility and love and safety

        the birds knew us
in the old languages
saw the love we were going to grow
        I collected
little branches from above our heads
a token of a sacred place
        it felt like
we were returning and being returned
to the land

that two women have laid together
under these trees
        always
and we were welcome once again

false gods

My palms promise love
secrets in these creases.
What can those stars tell us
distant cold spaces.
Everything happens in its proper way.
Hydrogen burns just so,
a fish can learn to breathe.
So it all moves on,
frozen seawater
to sand towns.
We're digesting plastic
spewing new life.
Cassowary nesting
beneath concrete overpass.
Cover your breasts
strong teeth from the bottle.
Calcifying, defying
Aquarian promises

pour rivers and streams   soak the dust.

To quiet   the night howls.

These indifferent stars   seen from above.

The emptiness   and fire

to make sense   of pink-cheeked bastards.

Dictating fortunes   from a pointed hat.

Dictating fortunes   it's easier to pray.

No time   for false gods.

We're burning, farming   in the new age.

Ancestral pathways   lead to tomorrow's pyre.

Adapting amongst the smoke   prepared by ancient hands.

dripping banksia pods

Boys hanging fists off the clothesline
for places I've never been and can never visit.
The rest is future.

Our clunking cheekbones
ringing mistakes my mind will play
over, a self-inflicted obsession

and some liberating kind of power.
I don't want to change the world, I just want to be there
giving out glances as bouquets.

Contempt for your then lover,
hubris in our footsteps.
Let me throw salt on your enemies,

let me warm you, darling,
pour milk on your heart
and a drop from my breast on each eye

to clear your vision.
He was the most beautiful thing I had ever seen –
Botticelli Michelangelo da Vinci.

Every word gospel,
every vision featured a blue-eyed beauty
dogmatic from another land.

So we learnt to live in a castle
landlocked and European. All I yearned for,
red dirt and forever air. What a gag.

Symphonic
spectral man suffering malaise
twisted light which moves around or through.

This town's a village, sitting with the
boys under olive trees
playing cards in torchlight

beneath the steeple, a churchyard glow.
Bullets lodged from some revolution inside
your mother's house. I run

dripping banksia pods, ectoplasmic
as I think of you in love
with legs and dimples and smells that aren't mine.

I ran from those soldiers
into the arms of women. They sing out
for me to drink freedom from their lips.

Time passing over a backyard fence rusting.
I'm safe here. Lover, you're pure light
shooting through someone else's skies.

touchable

t o u c h i n g
reaching   out
i l l u m i n a t i n g
your   face
with   my
f i n g e r t i p s
s c u l p t i n g
the   way
in   which
you   are
k   n   o   w   n
and   know
this   world
i l l u m i n a t e d
t o u c h a b l e
t o u c h i n g

heaven sent

Wattle blooms on the
    harshest days.

        /

      Every southerly will ease.

      The days are short
but the stars   are many.

      And you're all wrapped up in
             heaven

    /

           that thing I say
I don't believe in.

Since we met
      I forget there's a gloom
    of chilly days.

      Since we met   /
        I can only write love poems.

Since we met
      warm in your arms
    even the   coldest days
            are heaven sent.

yirawulin

the bush is glowing in the dying light

$$\qquad\qquad\qquad yirawulin$$

we're walking through trees scrub time cut stone

$$\qquad\qquad\qquad guwang\ dharama$$

the sky turning peach pink scarlet

$$\qquad\qquad\qquad warrungang\ warradagang$$

mist rising like fingers from the gorge

$$\qquad\qquad\qquad gadhalbar$$

and looking at all that sky

$$\qquad\qquad\qquad dhuran-dhurany$$

that's how I feel about you

$$\qquad\qquad\qquad guray-dyu-ngi-nya$$

the way the trees are sighing

      guray-marra-bi-rra

the mist in the still twilight air

      diranbirang

that's how I feel about you

      guray-dyu-ngi-nya

the birds in chorus

      gudyi

the song of running water

      yanggu

racing across the valleys

      barradambang

all this is how I feel about you

      guray-dyu-ngi-nya

stormgirl

she is the spark
            in the
                        tall dry
                        grass
hot summer nights
            a delicate
                        blend
of sweat and
            spit
            desire
and ant stings
                        the bitter crushed
                        scent
of a coming storm
                        red dust settles
tomorrow I am drought
today
            flooding rain

moreton bay fig

my moreton bay fig
forever roots mind
that ripple the
surface of
us two
some great
sea creature
breaching the soil
beneath our feet red dirt
feet work into red dirt grey
roots spiny backed lover
earthed your
self indispensable
earthing deep
immovable
ancient ridges
that flesh pressed
against remembers
cool grey
ridges of flesh
root stretching
to curl around
each other
wrapped
warm
red
dirt

phosphorescence

the water was clear
                the whole way down
and we were filled
              with the green light   of day   of life
we filled an ocean with life
and it shone
like the phosphorescence on our flesh
in the lightning storm in the creek that was all saltwater estuary
                    and I shone
with all the ways I yearned for you

old scars

I suppose

                I should say

I suppose

                I would

protect myself too

                from a lightly stepping

moon woman

                with red dust pouring

from her palms

                a trail to follow

I suppose

                it's only right to notice

the cruel star

                hiding in her smile

know that a storm is near

                a creature raises its wet nose

to the breeze

                catching the scent

of foreign dangers

                old scars warn of new storms

and they can warn of girls

                who float in on wicked zephyrs

I suppose

                it's only right to say I would notice

and I would say no

                but

I just don't think I would

                I just don't think I will

our weak constellations

I plot the fiery moments
that make up the stars

                        in our shared constellations
                    if only I'd never leant over and

kissed you at 5am
echoing door slams

                        of another woman's escape
               if only you'd not slipped into my bed

that next night
and every night thereafter

                        had not been so soft so
                        warm yearning tender

if you'd not cried in my arms
your eyes like spaceships

                        that I wanted to set free
                    from their celestial wanderings

I can chart the moments
that made me love you

                         and float past the dark patches
                              that overwhelm our skies

with my own tears
nights spent unslept

                                        sick with worry
                                   slick with other girls

with so much sorrow and shadow
I see our constellations

                         throw a weak light from here
                                            and I skip

from one star to the next
tracing my memories

                         wondering why I couldn't see
                              you could never love me

needles

I held the weave
of the cloth all
saffron and sky
in two hands
pressed the
weft upon
two lips
felt the
needles
within the threads
I pulled them from
our memories on hands
and knees I crawled
to feel every prick one
by one I amassed
a mountain of gold
a tower of banksia
glittery steps
that if only I
was brave
enough
or else
held no fear
could ascend
to kiss the pearl fish
the clouds and float
on currents
untouched

ripples

put your   tongue
between my   teeth
a new   silhouette
hot nights spent   unslept
instead   watching
a new   silhouette
which   breathes
a new   pace
my fizzing body   yields
moonlit cat   yowls
once again   undone
once again   begun

your mark
goes beyond my   beyond
                              flesh
                      two neat rows of
                                      indentations

            not piercing
though designed to
            not piercing today
                              a memory I can
                                      touch
      I see those teeth
marks upon my
                      speech my thoughts
                                      my self

I conduct my
    self with echoes
  of flesh

      echoes of your flesh upon
        my own

          pressed
            a jaw of neat
            fitting pearls

when we would lie
  heart to heart

    you're calcified within me
      a totem a talisman a chanting curse
  no longer
separate from the person

        we made

            within this
            echoing chamber

into the moonlight, away from me

you stepped into the moonlight

       away from me

smoke curling around

       the goddess line

from toes to crown

       I would pour resin

over your flesh

       to keep you trapped

in twilight

       this whispering house

softness turns

       you will dissolve with

that cigarette

       as you lean in darkness

a moon curve upon

       the doorframe

when you rise

       percolate

glowing

       to my touch

pepper

glass shattered around   our   mouths
I knelt to   collect the   petals
cut my fingers   upon the   weight   of
yourself a cat   running
soft   between my   legs
collecting night
collecting shadow
a cat
that laps   at the milk   upon our thighs
morning milk
congeals   and we are brushed   together
fragments   of two images   forced
when we make love   I   smell pepper
I push you   softer
I push you   sweeter
to hide   the   cracks
to   season the   wounds

a blue morning

if I gave you a blue morning
all air all lightness

like water from the stream
would you drink me

if I promised you
the true words for my love

the words that are carved upon
my bones

bones wet as a summer fling
but strong and true

would you cut your moon from sky
and come to the earthly plains of me

a silver line that waxes and wanes
under the quicks of my skin

darling I would turn the night
a blue thought a blue stone a blue star

I would walk
oyster sharp edge to flesh and cut

yourself down from the sky
stone to pearl

I will become a wellspring
of morning of us of us

I will turn in the air
I will return like the tide

to become the breath upon
your lips

and the waves
to which you wake

GUDYI

song

song for the rivers caring the land whole
carving the land together
whose currents birth us old here
BILA

song for the breeze who knows the shape
of my face turned skywards
fills these lungs with language and song
YAWILAWILAWIL

song for the soil who catches the tears
of our joy and our sorrow
blood and ash and possibility
DHAAGUN

song for the paths that lead us home
the scar trees that guide the way
holding safe ancestors and time and tomorrow
MURRU

song for the stone placed deep long ago
remembers the shape of the first land
and every hand whose touch wears it soft
MALANG

song for the the sun warm on our cheeks
mercy gift for life and destruction
who bends the will of a land dry and true
YIRAY

song for the rain whose gift heals the land
fills bila soothes dhaagun
flowing capacity of transformation
YURUNG

song for the places we digitally visit
while our physical limits keep us
untouched and together
GULUWIN

song for the land that cannot be claimed
mapped or stolen that withstands hard-footed herds
and agricultural poisons
GUYULGANG

song for Wiradjuri bila
song for Wiradjuri yawilawilawil
song for Wiradjuri dhaagun
song for Wiradjuri murru
song for Wiradjuri malang
song for Wiradjuri yiray
song for Wiradjuri yurung
song for Wiradjuri guluwin
song for Wiradjuri guyulgang
song for Wiradjuri gudyi

guwiiny-ngali-gin-dyi

away from here

guwiiny-ngali-gin-dyil

away from here

bila, a river cycle

what became of the river
who rose up
          and called themself human
stepped upon the land
containing the memories of snow melt and wellspring
          smooth worn stones along their ribs
and with water curiosity
sought to know more about the humans on the land
whose invasion of the waters choked the river

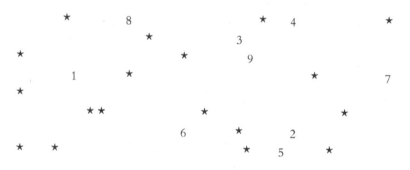

bila never sleeps for forwards for foreverness
for flow and gift and on and on …
and yet had become stagnant with
                    cruel touch a non touch and toxic intervention
dams rose where new humans demand
and irrigation sucks dry   to nourish not the plants of this land
but those with poisonous intent
yes the pesticides and all those carried in canola yellow plastics

in turn run this and that towards sweet water and so
             bila is transformed to the one you see today
                                              here la look la
to water not clear with flow and laughing bodies
                              small mouths and delicate fronds
but a sludge of gasping fish   carp muck   cow shit
                    don't drink from here no more no good
and when rain returns a moving sick comes across the land

                    —

             but a river is always a river ey even when submerged
             even dispelled even poisoned or damned
             cos spirits walk this land and ancestors placed bila
                         just so with cause of course

(ngarradan watched) (bilbi and giralang and dinggu watched)
(even bunyip waawii had not seen rivers walk upon two feet in
this world)

and so
             not dripping as the fish that leaps
but as a mist will rise from a dry river
                         so the mist turns solid rain
so bila became a human   skin shimmering a cool flesh green
             walks tumble glide over rocks
             or else some misted enormity
                    fish swim under skin
dangur flash of scale
along veins wrist and throat

yabi out of sight under
a lover can see in still morning light tails fins scales
dawn moon reflected in muck around
                    dropped branches collecting decaying
            damp cool flesh with the grey mud smell

(all folk love rivers   despite their erstwhile intentions
following in their mazdas nikes adidas

                              they follow where bila moves)
—

and bila moves now towards the sea
a cut stream known
by banks winding
                slow river ways and fast river ways
until under streets submerged a wide swamp of suburban delta
and the city appears upon aquifer disturbed
            water under concrete
                              through pipe and channel and drain
redirected rerouted and dispelled

                    yet   bila continues

        ★   8   ★   4   ★
                  ★   3
★   ★
        9   ★   ★
    1   ★   ★   7   ★

and so
what becomes of the river who flows out to see
what became of the people of the land
and what became of the river who rose up and
called themself human

a river is delight to behold all smooth and welcome with the flow
of places beyond horizon
and so too bila was in the form of
one climbing out of the beds and cars
of men women and all
trying to find people soft
trying to remember them as when
they leapt joy and free into cool depths splash of
hot day river sweet
saw the drops suspended in yellow light of blurred dream vision

a river can learn it all and still
must flow on and on to new mist and like the delta
where all is fertility and possibility
bila seeks the mangrove to clear the silt cycle
to move towards the sea
to dive into a world known as kin but always one hard to hold

to flow out and out to be reimagined as rain
and rejoin the lands of all rivers
of all stars
welcomed again into bilabang

1. bila – river
2. ngarradan – bat
3. bilbi – bilby
4. giralang – the stars
5. dinggu – dingo
6. waawii – bunyip
7. dangur – catfish
8. yabi – yabby
9. bilabang – a pool of water cut off from the river / the
   galaxy that contains our solar system, the 'Milky Way'

through the moon

I went out to watch the   moon rise
                    and was met by a horizon full of clouds
there's comfort in knowing she's there
            through this   through those clouds
                something like calling mum on the phone

/

I've always been impressed by people
who know about

                            meteors
                                    astroids
                            celestial movements

I've always been amazed by people
who can   close off their heart
                which is to say
                I find them awful

    the moon   is full tonight
but a sea of people   will fall asleep hungry
                    watched over by
                                        tides
                    stars
                        clouds
    that cannot feed
    that cannot mourn

/

        there is so much cruelty
that a pandemic
        swallows

                    crowds out
      the suffering of those in the light
forces many more   further into the dark

/

        I've always been impressed by people
who know about   the migration

                      of animals
                          of humans
             of birds
            who can read the tide
        or understand the trajectories

                    of a heart
why millions will walk   away from their homelands
      or back towards them
I've always been amazed by my privilege
              which is to say
             my ignorance disgusts me

/

        I'm calling to my mother

                  to the moon
          I'm calling home

through the clouds of a virus
                    that keeps me fixed in place
as I try to understand
                stars
                    birds
            human hearts

    I'm calling home
                  through the celestial objects I know
                  and through those I'm learning

I'm trying to say   I see you
            which is to say
                I see you through a computer screen
    which is to say
I'm blinded by   how little   I know

scatter gems

Scatter gems

                               collect

small hands small mouths

                         hollow children

to the breast.

                   Tend their wounds,

feed them ghee.

                        Thanks given

to those wrung dry.

                        Thanks given

shushing words

             a well of milk and cream

a poisoned tooth

                      or small cut

of decay

                     and place.

To curdled milk

              and maternal kindness.

my grandmother's spirit

I

My grandmother couldn't stay still.
She was possessed by a selfish spirit.

One that had to torture hearts,
a spirit that broke the glass in
every room.

The shards found their way
into my father's heart.

Those splinters worry the soles of my feet.

II

I look at my sibling and fear
for us.

Fear the demon waiting in our stolen shadows.

The voice that moves us. Selfish.

The eyes looking beyond the horizon
ears straining at the cracks.

Wondering where the next whole heart
meal awaits.

III

I never met my grandmother, the topic
rarely crossed our kitchen table or
long car drives.
Trauma is a secret keeper.

But I feel her red dust legacy
in my itching fingertips. I feel her

running in ripples around me, hear
her selfish whispers.

IV

I understand you,
I say to the ghost,

I know what spirit possessed you

through those flyscreen doors
in the middle of the night.

I know which stars in the crashing still dark
guided you,
over flat dry riverbed country.

V

That spirit is in my blood stream.
Floating in this air on a windless night.

and as oil spreads across still water
the waves of smallpox-blistered bodies could not be stopped
a death begun by the white hand
without needing to touch the gun

/ the times were unprecedented /

and flour bags of rationed poison
stole whole families of their life
a stitched government insignia
the last image before their clouding eyes

/ the times were unprecedented /

and when the sacrosanct of elsewhere
exported their fears of anyone
not male not white not them
a sickness of the mind snatched the sacred vision of all bodies

/ the times were unprecedented /

and when the angry blacks travelled
in 1938 to the place called sydney
to hold signs for a day of mourning
for their human rights to dignified existence

/ the times were unprecedented /

and when the first queer victims began to burn
with HIV spreading like fire through their cells
abandoned and vilified
as we lost the most beautiful of a generation

/ the times were unprecedented /

and to all bodies
who have feared their government
the four walls of their house
or a world not designed for them

/ these times are precedented /

a case study of the colony

a case study of the colony – in lutruwita (tasmania) – twentytwenty (in the year of the coloniser). a property called cullenswood (we know that's not the true name of that place) / was sold for twelve million dollars (in the colonisers' currency). after six (one two three four five six) generations of the legge family (who never bought the land / but certainly spilt blood enough to call it theirs) ///

back then (and how long ago it was!) those first legge – after never making a purchase to this place (not guided by their own far-off law) – marched across the land and tore from the earth any person who would remember the land's true name. and those they could not kill fled – followed by hordes of hard-footed hard-mouthed square-eyed animals (they took from the soil all things – and in turn the humans would profit from the wools the meats the young). from the soil too they would seed those plants (those plants with the same origins as the legge) lace the soil with plants that poison the land slowly like a sickness spreading. plant it out and sell that too ///

not satisfied with the surface next they would open wounds across the land. great open sores into the earth called mine. mine mine mine – a word foundational to a people who can take from others a thing they call mine. they cut the hole (mine) and took from the ground what couldn't be seen on the surface. stories that swim with ancient fish in quartz-coloured streams underground. they took all that (those spirits of the land where minerals lie) ///

72

maybe they felt unsettled or like winds they couldn't see moved across their souls. the legge built a church (of a far-off religion) and in this faith they built a yard to place bodies (bodies of their own only) buried in neat wooden boxes made of strong local timber (placed within that blood-soaked land) ///

the legge spread out from the place they named cullenswood and when a legge saw a bird or a mountain or some thing that made them feel some way they named it for themself (legge mountain) (legge eagle) as though these things did not have names given to them since before time began – as though these things were not true things that existed before legge. the name spread far and the people of cullenswood said aren't you glad the legge were here ///

and when there was nothing left to kill – contaminate – extract – they sold the place (that system of wealth that means a thing stolen can be sold) and when they sold it they said – we are the people of this land. six generations (one two three four five six legge) the time it takes two lives to begin and end and the memories run clear. the thing that wasn't bought can be sold and can be sold on a bloodless deed (for the paper remembers a border drawn and not the bodies who fell) these civilised people put it into law that death without looking over their shoulder. and the colony said oh those people who were here didn't know how to use the land and it wasn't theirs anyway and ///

no what people before? we are the people of

the cullenswood and that is the name of the land.

keep in touch

now children,   it's time to begin the rotations

I

yellow light

step upon this timber floor   you remember this place
                    practice
          recite along the line
                    you know this homely institution

II

the body makes the mark
                    which is the mark
can you feel the dough in your hand?   *touch*
the first sense   haven't found the words yet
          the form is   *pre-lingual*
breathing, drying
                    the shape begins to solidify

III

tasting   to learn the world
          everything here   *for safe consumption*

IV

patchwork

who's that crowning through
mummy's big cunt?
the pattern is moving   *but*
you recognise running through a world full of knees, soft fabrics
        unknown faces   the skirt tells you you're home
the caretaker is soft

        the touch is   *childhood memory*
        the print is   *cultural memory*
    we've commenced your phase of

                                lingual expression
everything to plan
for now, you are safe

V

reaching for the hand   fleshy (but with glass)
the dough which holds the touch   *yields*
        speaks to the hand   alone without the body
tender affection

        how should you reach to reciprocate?

VI

group time!
to understand this part, we must mark it
the concept of time   *learn this*
                is abstract

we quantify it   to qualify it

you're beginning to be   *institutionalised*

it's not so bad though   societal reality

VII

quantifying memory   repetition helps

        repetition helps   move to fairytale to learn this part

see these pumpkins

(you may have to look hard)   they're hiding in your

        cultural memory

        (remember?)

grotesque goldilocks all wrapped up in scarf and cloth

        object impermanence

will be overcome

VIII

gathered around the fire   a continuation of the fairytale

        it may be convenient here

to remember the motherland   (which mother?)

make it a fireplace   *sentimental*

a place for breaking bread

have you noticed?

        the mother is absent, the story is take

        pay attention

IX

are you feeling big now?

the dough has turned to stone
time to wash away the play!   shimmery pink soap
does it remind you   of the caretaker's pink hands?
                    mummy polystyrene
                    grandmother's glass
this is a fire you can
          touch

X

from precognition then
                    we could not feel   what had been held
the mark upon the dough

                              the absent form remembers
speaks of then
mark making   to mark time   *to now*
                    memory creates the object
                    a residue left behind
together
we have moved through all the steps   full of tricks
and how familiar the space is!

PS

          unlearning is a long journey home

my hand is a bird

My hand is a bird I raise to my mouth
        to feed
           in a gesture of peace
To your mouth I break these fingers
           in love

      One day he will wear
         a gown
      That I have sewn
         with my
      hair instead of cloth

         Wearing
      my menstrual blood
         to remember
      a mother's ocean weeps
      To watch you walk away

My hand is a bird I raise to my mouth
To your mouth I break these fingers
to feed
a mother's ocean weeps
in a gesture of peace

One day he will wear
my menstrual blood
That I have sewn
in love
to remember

To watch you walk away
Wearing
a gown
with my
hair instead of cloth

smoke of the middens burning
to make the limestone to make the mortar
build fortresses
to hold the lies strong

a woman quaking

I am rising, falling,

                    transforming,

my earth is shaking,

          the blood is stirring.

I watch from above

          hues and shades I didn't

anticipate;

               making my fingers

itch, my feet quake

               wading into this river

of strange lovely fish.

Upstream, dam unstuck

cool water soaks

          a forgotten dry valley

is filled with life

          the world in colour.

I see myself, almost

               overcome by

a million ripples

          set in motion by

tiny moments, tiny pebbles.

          (I didn't notice

their fall,

          didn't hear the drop,

yet all around me

               water stirs.)

I am rising, falling,

          transforming.

Oh, what a wonderful thing

          to be a woman quaking.

galaxies and nothing at all

(or) side by side, I ask what are you thinking about?

You're thinking about 'galaxies and
nothing at all'

indifferent cosmic places,
that's an awful lot of nothing.

And I'm thinking about my
husband

who's earthly
and not here.

We're remnants of a superb explosion
every step choreographed

by a universe so distant
so full of care.

Fission and fusion
that lead to you and me

and us and them
and all those other

complexities
fizzing, fusing.

I wrestle with the sun
to see more

from my tiny corner
in all this.

We're all made of the same
star stuff that moved me

lying next to
an undiscovered universe

moved by dust
gases and carbon

and still more dust. And dust,
the same old stuff.

Stars aligned and here we lie
thinking about galaxies

and nothing.
Everything

and nothing.
Out of all that silence

what nothing are we
to this endless galaxy?

salvation of the new world

your grandmother has patterns
along her eyes that you can
trace with your finger

> your grandfather is a star being
> he will return there
> back to the constellations

these hands are stirring
against a body stained with ink
memories of a family

> can he see you now
> does he shift the cosmos
> in your favour

this city is lit from within
sophisticated circuits
and delighted patterns

> an oasis
> shimmering and false
> it outshines us

and while we're adrift on this quickening tide
I'm happy just being far from home
in the orbit of your cosmos

let us suppose

(let us suppose, on some still night,
yes, a humid night a lot like this one)

We climb up the rusting ladder,
Mexican beer forced into waistbands,
and lie on the cooling roof
count our personal galaxies
far high LEDs, billboards, dreams.
You won't get aggressive from the booze tonight
but sweet, softly blurred around the edges.

And let's suppose we begin to make promises,
the far-reaching ones that reflect our age
and all the impossible potential held in our humid thighs
and starry eyes.
We compare shadows and the blue glow
of distance. Scattering sweetly scented flowers
around an impossible future.
I would see these tears as art
and so we would be.

You lie in that shiny black
wet hot seed. I yearn to plant and feast
the vines that strangle stubborn feet.
Soft brown lips
sometimes stirring, like dozing lovers
on your dozing lover face.

High above the street lights. Two impossible galaxies
upon their backs, comparing the tyranny of future.
Of course, distance doesn't apply to warming bodega beer.
Until we drift and dissolve
back to this moment.
Soft and young, again we will meet,
in tropical filthy rain, we retreat.

bushfire love
(on realising there is no home here)

and then
all of a sudden
and with really
no warning
those dreams
in which I had sat
so safe
the feathers
with which I dressed
my nest
I found cinders
where I had fed
silken parrots
I saw
sparrows perhaps
pigeons surely
were wearing our clothes
were hiding in my eyes
in parrot's dress
we swept up
the ash
that fell like snow
between us
on your lashes
on my bones
grey feathers
of home

I wept red sand
   those sparrows
      began to starve
        in their painted feathers
         to reveal ash
           grey feathers
            not the red
              of home
sand filled
   our grey soviet flat
     that nest of ash
       to swamp our windows
        dust appeared
         in the cracks
           we could not hold back
 a desert that grew
   between these walls
     and still I wept for
       I never meant to starve
        amongst this flock
         never meant to
   sing for ash
     never knew the power
      of red sand
        how the song of home
         could overwhelm
          a love of parrots

a cab, early morning, in the rain

Lilac sky swollen
lights. A slick black car on
slick black roads.

Stars don't shine in this town
only satellites,
humankind's wandering wonders.

I'd rather wish on circuits
than lost black stars.

Your salty swollen lips
underbite overheard
and the overpass green glow
where shadows
tessellate upon your face
swallowing you, again.

Though, of course,
your face is
a clear wet horizon.

We're more likely
to wash away in the stormwater,
than share these
hot green dawns.

oil afloat at birrarung marr

that rainbow slick
will drift beautiful
and toxic far away
from here from
us and kill
far away
from here
from
us

.

a
stand
of tall gums
my mother's
wood-smoke house
I count the leaves home
and dream of other trees
follow the oil slick out
to sea together we
infect dolphins
and anemones
to wash up
upon the
same old
shores
again
again
again

I don't sleep anymore

I don't sleep anymore
instead I feast with my arms
deep to the elbows
in the primordial stickiness of hope
from it I pull many fevered sicknesses
and a constant series of doors
but it's not like the metaphor where a window opens
it's more like a dimensionless maze
and some hydra beast

I don't sleep anymore
instead I plant seeds throughout the moon garden
and wait for my children to rise up
from the twin wombs in our bed
the place where I whisper and chant
for peace

I don't sleep anymore
instead I dream of places where I can step upon the ground
and not hear the cries of kin rising from blood-soaked earth
shrinking beneath a mean sky

no I don't sleep anymore
I just weep and weep
until I turn back to a river

no I don't sleep anymore
now I wander through the smoke plume
inhaling the dust of that
long distant explosion

I don't sleep anymore
instead I dance with my eyelids
deep to the moon
in the sun of a primordial light
from it I pull many fevered children
and a constant many-coloured wail
~~but~~ it's ~~not~~ like the metaphor where a path forks
but more like an ailing animal
forgetting pain

I don't sleep anymore
instead I shake dust throughout the dream garden
and cry for my children against time
from the seeds in our hearts
the place where I spin and spin
and weep

I don't sleep anymore
instead I visit places where I can step with the ancestors
and find peace in my kin rising from the earth
hoping beneath an endless song

no I don't sleep anymore
I just laugh and laugh
until I turn back to a child

no I don't sleep anymore
now I wait for you upon the shore
inhaling the oyster shells of that
long distant ocean

ngulumunggu

endings

digital native

yeh I'm native — ones and zeros — digital —
babe I can tell you about the ways that code
and poetry intertwine — all these deliberate
interventions — all this data — big census numbers
— little pixels long strings — how they count up
the natives — and yeh but who's counting — ones
and zeros ones and zeros — do we take spears
through the digital frontier — hear the rattles in the
server — do we rain dance the cloud and ask for
the numbers back — ones and zeros zeros and ones
— how does it feel when the cloud bursts —
zerooneonezerooneonezerooneonezerozerozeroone
they're 3D printing ceremony now — dot dot dot
painting 1080 pixels — and the RAP banner image
is always stock hands dot in the sand cos no one
wants to pay but they'll take some cultural credit
paypal afterpay donate here — ancestral data bank —
sacred in the server — babe we've always been in the
network — we are the network — of course it's black
the whole way down — ones and zeros — yeh babe
I'm a digital native — I guess we're all native now
oneoneonezerooneonezerozerooneonezerooneezeroone

time travel

memory swings back   / round
time is time travel to places
               where I can re
                       write
the way it was done

          tree rings   travel too
drought and smoke fire
               sing in the fingertips
of time to take our water bodies
                   back to water

        if I go   forward
another time travel in mind
but forwards to see her or him
          explore to see why
               but why not
so we come back to
               now

to fix up the dance /   steps
returning
          to breath and fire

maybe adjust the past
          push a flood or a woman ahead
a few steps to make sense of
             narrative

and a conversation in which you explained
          what you really felt

                              when you said
no time is real all time is time travel
          all travel is time   shifting
today is tomorrow over there
                              / or is it yesterday /

from tall stilts those wide-mouthed humans
          watch as we wander
                    wonder about direction
compass hearts travel laterally
          when of course we should float above
seeing forwards and back   /   janus-faced lover
understands the myth of tomorrow

                              the myth of past
fingering the monsters back

if you float below the soil
          and see through
there is no time
/   the rocks stack horizontal
     tilting towards light
it seems
to let the truth in
          we both know all time is
                              time travel

the transit of venus

I

a vessel to follow a goddess
stinking boards and mouths with rot
floggings of one in five
odds are high
to never set foot upon sand soil loam

and yet
as though by god given grace
that ship through storms
more stars to follow

as disease to the pearly flesh
that tears through the idle
idyllic isle
it's all green cast ashore
a paradise of course

tahiti

twenty miles across and the time so vast
yet square white clouds
a waking nightmare come real with brass buckles
telescopes and fine shining lenses

here yes that goddess promise of
love beauty sex desire
emerges from a grand clamshell

98

the cries of her kind hidden in night
but fertility with sickness
that plants a deep seed
does venus only love a white woman

II

a small black spot and the three-pointed hat
failed to quantify the stars
a false transit

but in the small scrawl footnote
stamp and seal with crown
another goddess is promised
hidden lands to scorch and claim

terra australis incognita

what lead to the goddesses of your skies
to guide by night to this shore
our stars speak of all time
they wake in the east and chase a sky long
here the whole world is enough

venus goddess of war
whose brand of love brings fire
steel poison and flagpole
brunt again soft skulls
sailing forth
boiling water deep underground

III

the reef is a fertile loving expanse
graciousness looks like calcification
a million pulsing polyps
no soft white cheek and glittering advancement

a furthering endeavour
snatching hands collect seeds and grains
rope and basket
a never forgotten
foul ship first theft
and promise of an empty land

cook was unsure down to the forty-second second
and no crown could own the size of the sky
but a transit
the end of many worlds
the first ghosts of a pox ridden army
landing upon shell shores

                                    great britannia

transit for glory
without a captured star
but poles that grow from greed
flag of strange relation
to end the world

and a great hungry mother
guiding to war
venus was a traitor to the south

on sun-days

on sun-days
we assemble, cheering
in bloodlust, in fear
warm crowds
leaning in, pushing out
to become crows
we always were
feasting on carrion

warm crowds
feasting on carrion
in bloodlust, in fear
we assemble, cheering
        on Sun-days
we always were
leaning in, pushing out
to become crows

leaning in, pushing out
warm crowds
we assemble, cheering
feasting on carrion
to become crows
we always were
in bloodlust, in fear
        on sun-days

desert places

Desert places,
    filled with life

I see as I exhale you, pink
    flowers bloom as I

breathe you in I
    forget myself,

lost in red sand, warmth
    doesn't flow, it explodes.

Tomorrow I will question my resolve.
    Tomorrow rain will come.

The beat of another heart is no
    compass, for three and four

and many more beat not as
    one but

a deafening cacophony,
    desert song.

Desert places, searching for life.

prayer is electric

I

magic is a transfer of energy
prayer is electric
something about human bodies
made of water
conduit things

II

tea-tree leaves
to clean the wound
fire to prepare the loam
bottlebrush
to sweeten the water

III

there was a funnel-web spider
in our lounge room '98
out back
my dad was growing pot
he couldn't even make money
selling drugs

IV

the doctor told me when I was
nineteen that I have
problematic ovaries

she said it might be an issue
if I ever wanted to get pregnant
I wasn't confident I knew the answer to
the question
so I stopped visiting that doctor
to avoid knowing more

V

I burn from the inside
the pain shifts around
eludes the cause
I don't want to hold coals inside
wouldn't wish it on

VI

I find it very hard to focus my
thoughts
on my real father
they whip about
between pity and pain
some shimmering obligation of love

VII

I have a photograph of my father
as a toddler
on my wall
I can't hate a toddler
with smooth full cheeks
a bulging pocket with
perfect glass marbles inside

the careful knitted jumper
no, I can't hate this toddler
with his little koori dimples
on three rivers country

VIII

so if I can't hate the toddler
how can I hate the man he will become
we're all born innocent

IX

mountain rose will ease an aching heart
I know remedies of another people
but can't make a dough from
wattle seed
don't know the properties of
bottlebrush banksia
don't even know their names

X

my father had a knack for
knowing plants

XI

I can't separate where things begin

XII

it's hard to carry magic
in a town like his
it's easy to get hard or
turn the other way
it's a good idea to leave on the wind
blown from desert towards the coast
but where to go

XIII

red dust woman
bruises form
to boy to man

XIV

I wish he'd been a better man
my father
I wish he'd been easy to love

XV

prayer is electricity
the human body is water
we can find wells in the desert
sing for rain
to wash away the dust

the young men are singing

the young men are singing along the bridges of the city
                                                    wearing face masks
            they're walking into the highways
                                    eyes to the sky
six lanes stopping to hear their songs

            the young men and the birds
                        will rise up in their chorus
to gather below the moon
                                    translucent
                        dissolving in the milky glow

the steel scaffolds and iron harnesses of the grid
            will soften
                        dissolving into song
wherever notes swell or those gentle fingers touch

and slowly the city will rise
            into the air
                        into the mist

                        a mirage of yellow cranes
            unfinished sky scrapers
mismatched wires dangling below the exposed concrete belly

the birds will stay below
                        two legged
            to pick at the naked insects left behind
at the edges of the flattened grass

hot and cold

she's hot and cold
and she breaks my heart
I know there is someone else

I know I should run
for the fucking hills
but I swear

if you could see this
sleeping face
all carved stone softness

a pin-up
from outer space
from the desert

a rose
under glass
helen of fucking troy

to launch my aching body
my aching heart
into her soft arms

she blooms a smile
abandoned last night
but this morning

I crawl against her warmth
she murmurs whispers kisses
my heart

is breaking
in these arms
but I swear

if you could see this face
you would let your heart
be broken

again this morning
to believe the lies
and kiss those lips

sip deception
from her neck
and curse yourself

for looking at that face
for crawling into those arms
for letting her break your heart

again

the space between the paperbark

when we fuck I time travel
I enter the space between the paperbark
soft tannins
I climb underneath the ash

apathy

and all of a sudden I looked and saw nothing   the fly that wriggles into the ear
    while you are blissfully unaware   sleeping perhaps or else
                distracted by sunlight   caught in the edge of a
                                spider's web and you wonder   lazily
why a human world   bothers   to swat down   a masterpiece
        and so the fly   which crawled into your ear
                        while you pondered the web   or maybe you were asleep
                            its shimmery poison into your   unsuspecting blood stream
has had time to drop
        a poison   of lethargy of time
                and all of a sudden I look at you and   I see nothing

that shore which is a cliff

looking back
once there's a view
and everything settles
into ordered place
cogs of fine clocks
that work like silver fish
wonderful clever lines where
seashells precisely litter the shore
and time and wind and dust
fall like stars
stars caught in your hair
dancing on your tongue
confusing the proper from
their path into ravines guiding
the wayward back to light
my darling
we stand
upon that shore
that shore which is a cliff
a strange and beautiful horizon
I still love you because you set me free

how to make a basket

time weaves a horizon of many strands

the end of the world was marked with beautiful light
we should have known
as mega fires surrounded the city
and our leaders lounged
off shore on beach with shandy in hawaiian print

we marvelled
the orange air more brilliant and terrifying
than an instagram filter
our skin glowed and glowed as the horizon
and we were together to watch it burn

retying grass knots
again again again

the age of the idealised self
didn't touch our fingertips
the sun hung heavy angry near in a thick sky
we choked
our photographs were perfect

we looked beautiful at the end of the world
and the content was fire
the lighting was golden the lighting was lit
how predictable that the end of the world
would be captured in a selfie

                    the sun gets hotter as it ages
          we're dreaming we're dreaming of a cold young sun

when smoke hangs low over the city basin
it is a new town another town
one wearing death as a halo
or else revealing itself
as a place where wicked things can occur

this Country is not bad
but bad happens here
hear the smoke curl around the monuments
trying to reclaim sovereign stone

we burn leaves to cleanse a place
                but this
I wouldn't call this smoke
a healing medicine

                        willie wagtails are not nocturnal
                        but they will sing to the moon
                        I will call her dyirridyirri

follow to the end of the street
and remember small fires in the gorge
each one that used to be safe
each one that used to be a family

                        I climb underneath the ash

my Country is beyond the horizon
all plains all river
the edges can be crossed with care
            you might say the language is
harsh
but it is an ancient beauty
a life that rolls and sings

                          and we're singing we're singing

I wake up to a woman
wading through tall birds
heart-shaped leaves
with perfect breasts that hang
long and heavy
scars along her chest

                              her basket is safety

everything worth holding in two hands
has a perfect basket to respond

                        how to make a basket

first you must begin
with the grasses
first you must tend the blades
the sweet small shoots
first you must make healthy the soil
care for this place

tend with fire
carry the seeds
first you must make the land right
first you must love your mother

                    what you care for will care for you

when you are ready
you will understand
how to make a basket

notes

All Wiradjuri language in *how to make a basket* began with learnings from *A New Wiradjuri Dictionary* by Uncle Stan Grant Snr and Dr John Rudder. Any errors in this book are totally my own.

'sweet smoke' is written for and dedicated to the Djab Wurrung Embassy and their fight for sacred land.

'gungunga' tells a story set on Gweagal land, when Captain Cook set foot on an ancient land and claimed it in the name of another.

'to fanny cochrane smith, to whale breath' is dedicated to lutruwita Tasmania and especially to the memory of Aunty Fanny Cochrane Smith, whose song continues to ring out and fight back.

'gully song' was written within and about The Gully in Katoomba on Darug land. 'A good fire will trickle across the land like water' comes from a speech Victor Steffensen gave in 2019.

'we rise' is after Hannah Brontë's 'Still I Rise' (2016), which is after Maya Angelou.

'listen' was written in response to the 2020 NAIDOC theme 'Always Was, Always Will Be'.

'/ unprecedented times / 2020' is dedicated to those never lost, to those we keep losing.

'a case study of the colony' is a response to the sale of the 'Cullenswood' property in lutruwita Tasmania in 2020. The real estate listing advertised that the land was for sale for 'the very first time' and listed a manor home, grazing pasture, an open-cut coal mine, timber logging plantation, water catchment storage, a cemetery and a church. No history before the Legge family occupied the site was mentioned.

'keep in touch' began as a response to a conversation with artist Alice McIntosh. It then shifted and twisted to become 'the new place', published by *Overland* in 2020.

'I don't sleep anymore' is a line adapted from Natalie Diaz's 'From the Desire Field' which opens with 'I don't call it sleep anymore'.

'digital native' is inspired by Indigenous Data Sovereignty, a movement critical for our people.

'prayer is electric' was written on Turtle Island with guidance from Lumbee medicine learnings.

'the young men are singing' is a borrowed and mangled line from Federico García Lorca's 'Ode to Walt Whitman' which opens 'Along the East River and the Bronx, the young men were singing'.

'hot and cold' is after Dorothy Porter.

'how to make a basket' was written during the Black Summer tragedy of 2019–2020. It is indebted to Amanda Holroyd's print 'Mayi Ngamparam' (2015).

mandaang guwu, thank you

To you, dear reader.

To this continent, the many nations I have called home, and to the Elders across this land who continue to keep Country and mob strong. In particular, mandaang guwu to Uncle Stan Grant Snr and Dr John Rudder, whose preservation of the Wiradjuri language has been a path down which I continue to walk back to culture.

To all the First Nations poets, storytellers, activists and artists of this continent who have written, sung and shouted before me. To all the matriarchs without whom none of this would be possible.

To Cammeraygal land of the Eora where I was born, Gundungurra and Boon Wurrung Countries where I was raised. To my adult homes upon the lands of the Wurundjuri, Gadigal, Dja Dja Wurrung, Gundungurra and Darug, where much of this book was written. And beyond this continent to Munsee Lenape of Turtle Island; the lands of the Molalla of the Confederated Tribes of the Grand Ronde of Turtle Island; Budapest, Magyarország; and Marpha in the Lower Mustang, Nepal – places where this collection was seeded, grown and harvested.

To the First Nations and queer communities that keep this world beautiful and my life abundant.

To my beautiful, huge, loving family. To my mother. To Elijah, Lucy, Rebecca, Justin.

To my darling (almost) wife Jen, thank you for weaving this life with me.

And to the loves before, with apologies for the moments I have cannibalised into this collection.

Thank you to all the gorgeous friends, far too many to name here. And to Ivy, for being the best.

Thank you to the State Library of Queensland and the 2020 judges of the David Unaipon Award for this big life-changing award. To Ellen, who helped refine the weave of this basket. To Aviva for the guiding hand. To Cathy and Yasmin for the sharpest eyes. To Jenna for the perfect cover. To Natalie, Yvette, Omar and Tony for your kindnesses.

To the different prizes for poetry, the encouragement and endorsement from winning or being shortlisted has been immense and I am so grateful to: University of Canberra Aboriginal and Torres Strait Islander Poetry Prize, Nakata Brophy Poetry Prize, Oodgeroo Noonuccal Indigenous Poetry Prize, Val Vallis Poetry Prize, Peter Porter Poetry Prize, and the Aunty Kerry Reed-Gilbert Poetry Prize.

Thank you to the Australia Council for the Arts, Rosehips Foundation in Marpha, Nepal, Varuna Writers' House and Copyright Agency.

To the editors and curators of the various journals, anthologies and exhibitions where different poems from within this collection have previously appeared, this book could not exist without the tireless efforts of those who love, commission and believe in poetry. Thank you: *Artist*

Profile, *Australian Book Review*, *Australian Poetry Anthology*, *Australian Poetry Journal*, *Borderless* (Recent Works Press), *Blacklight* (Sweatshop), *Collective: Ghost*, *Cordite Poetry Review*, Emerging Writers' Festival podcast, First Nations Australia Writers Network, Firstdraft, *Lieu Journal*, *Liminal*, *Meniscus*, Murray Art Museum Albury, *Overland*, *No News* (Recent Works Press), Queen Victoria Women's Centre, *Rabbit*, *Runway Journal*, Sister zine, *Westerly* and *West Space Offsite*.